THE ART OF MAKING STONE
LOVE STONE
POEM COLLECTION

For every artist realizing love . . .

and the struggle to do so . . .

Barbara L. McBee

ISBN 978-1-957220-03-1 (paperback)
ISBN 978-1-957220-04-8 (hardcover)
ISBN 978-1-957220-05-5 (digital)

Copyright © 2021 by Barbara L. McBee

All rights reserved. No part of this publication may be reproduced, distributed, or transmitted in any form or by any means, including photocopying, recording, or other electronic or mechanical methods without the prior written permission of the publisher. For permission requests, solicit the publisher via the address below.

Rushmore Press LLC
1 800 460 9188
www.rushmorepress.com

Printed in the United States of America

Contents

Acknowledgment v

Against a crack in time 1
Balloon 2
It was the first day of spring 3
Ode to spirit 6
A feather wafted across my path 9
A fern 10
A great ship majestic of sail 11
If tenderness were a flower 12
1001 14
birth 15
Black smoke. Tossing 16
The case of the missing spirit 18
Cataclysms 22
Charcoal chartreuse 24
Come here 25
Fall 27
February blues 28
First snow 29
How do you put out a fire 30
I am not at home 31
I grieve you 33
I thought I heard your voice in 35
I wanted it 37
If I open like a flower 39
If you lost yourself in me 40
In the spirit of decoration 41
It is bluer than I imagined 42

Like a delicate brulee crust	44
Listen to her spirit	45
Lucky seven	47
Melancholy is a good word	48
It is Monday	49
A chill slid across my heart and this harbinger tore open a stream of assaults	50
Ocean	51
My table is filled	53
offering	55
One, two, three	56
Poem one and two	57
Today is a special day	58
Prestige	60
Red	61
Curled across a chest	62
She was a treasure	63
Sorcerer	65
Special delivery	66
Spring and the feathers floated across the yard	67
Stop here, she said	68
The call	70
The end of an era	71
The photos have no meaning	72
I can turn three minutes into	74
Under the deep	76
Under the magnolia tree	77
Under the boxwood	78
The unmade bed	80
Volcanic ash spewed	82
You digest	84

Acknowledgment

For every artisan realizing love . . . is within and around you . . . everywhere you look . . .

For Phyllis . . . for my mentor Daisaku Ikeda, a true warrior of the pen . . .

May you find great joy from within.

Against a crack in time

Pounded against a crack in time

I was catapulted through an unopen door

I met myself; I met a rush of unspeakable courage and daring

A light was lit in the house of rooms gone empty and dormant

A gust of wind blew a scrap of old newspaper around on the dusty floor

I unfolded it and it was moist and good as new

The date was a thousand years ago

There was no headline because it was a slow day that year

When conversation meant more to each of us and you could still smell snow coming when you lifted your eyes to the sky

I heard a tingle in the bell that rang in my heart it grew to a fierce clanging but the clacker sent it round

Reverberating against that unopened door came the offering of sound so resonant the walls bled

Tears

The walls bled tears dripping across that old headline and I smelled snow and salt

From a thousand years ago

October 22, 2013

Balloon

I jumped in deep water

Not having been there before, my guides took me quietly

Indigo opened to a silver pathway, a school rushed by

A light revealed the harpoon's score and life and death side by side enveloped me

Alone, connected to a source, I always knew I traveled again to an open field

Yellow flowers waved high atop this mountain and my hair was filled with them

Watching the sky in air so lilting I inhaled

Covered in gold arms full of intricate bangles, my belly covered in roses, I inhale the gifts left across my toes

Standing at a precipice in my black dress, the room goes on without me as I enter under cloak of lace and suede cinch

I glide through like deep water struggling to blend in or hang on to what I have gained in this explosion of

Color and air and salty sea

I am two and running through my grandmother's yard

Balloon

October 22, 2013

It was the first day of spring

Not just any other day

Grass grew, nest-building occurred

And a soft lilt in the wind halted my attention

Minor easily dismissed

A hum underneath the crackling of still soggy winter leaves and broken plastic

A tiny hum, not sure

Was it

I leaned in, tomorrow it said

Today, most likely

Of yesterday, no need no need

More need than one could imagine

I yawned gaping, gaping so roundly I frightened myself

Gaping here and then

The wound was largely visible

I could bake fill the hole with food and share it with someone who was also hungry

I could whip a soufflé with my injured wrist until it was exhausted

In that exhaustion, I could forget as the eggs ran across my jaw and

I licked the spoon wondering if there was more

A pause, a brief pause, I pondered brownies instead deep black sticking to my gums

I would know they were there. I would fight to get rid of them

Caramel, oh caramel, you stick endlessly I am reassured

Instead, I listened. With every ounce of my life force, I listened

And only heard the sound of my tears

Tears of relief, tears flooding down my cheek repeatedly, a mockery of my life

I tried to laugh. I tried to stop listening. I tried to consider the next recipe

I tracked my own photographs for traces of myself. My eyes betrayed me

As did others

I searched endlessly inside myself and I recalled a sunrise in the rain—

A sunrise that was clear

A sunrise that reminded me of fresh manure that gave life and fruit and holiest of things

I love that smell comforting in its sticky putrid vulgar warm possibility of life

I looked for it now out of the muck I slung over my shoulder. I searched for it

Digging, digging, slamming into shale hardest rock, I would have it. I would watch it grow

I searched and listened to the tiny sound of something green and frail pushing itself up from the shale where roots reached into the center cavity of putrid muck

It was spring only spring and I heard it loud and clear—

Hope

March 22, 2014

Ode to spirit

It is the thing of mysterious intangibility

That steps carefully across ponds, rocks, sidewalk cracks

Suspended wholly, reachable in rain and dark nights

Under moons by wolf's howl

It is red, maybe it is green

Sometimes it is blue because I am

In all that, it means to be longing or joyous or tremendously rich of it

And for it

It is the kindest wrap one can wear in fall's mourning colors of rebirth

Each crispy leaf a memory to the springtime to follow

A husky breath in the cold imprints its colors in the air

Frozen in time, I can revisit it at leisure daily

Examine it for clues or view it by kaleidoscope

I can warm myself with it or use it for a stepping stone on my walk on the beach when the water laps too high past my ankles

The softest slipper by firelight illuminated or lost in the darkness in caves where only I can resurface renewed

It is complete in and of itself though the costumes vary moment to moment, year to year, lifetime to lifetime

To be shared or kept sealed tight . . . can a flower grow under glass?

Would it know it is dwarfed to its sister or is it enough to flourish there?

In and out weaving through the crowds of them . . . do you recognize each other in travels by dawn or dusk?

On fair isle and port, by desert or high across a mountain plateau, where a breeze whispers the name of the town you are in today

A prescription for evening, a tonic by day, will waft across the plateau, staining it with song and dance

It smiles and changes course for the moment, undaunted, undeterred, with this shred of kindness and beauty

A butterfly, a blind bee with a job to send a message to a flower that waits expectantly in the dark

It is all those things in a beloved way. It is none of those things in a way equally as loved

Is it viewed by air or in the wafting of heat that rises on the freeway at noon and leaves a ripple in the blacktop?

Must it have a name in the first place? Must it say it? Must it say it? Must it reveal the nature of it? As it is all of nature—in her orange shoes and red dress or the studs on her belt and the crown she wears of victory and loss and hunger and such sweet secrets that have no name, no realization, no answer

They simply are in the drifting and the daydreams and the reveries and the dust

It simply is and will always be

There is no answer to why it cannot be said because there is no question for it

Real

I touched it so I know I saw it depart once or twice. I nearly lost it on several occasions but it returned with a toss of hair and a raucous laugh. I was tricked into believing time was up

There is no end, there is no end, there is no end

Beyond the borders of what I know, it is not possible

There is always another day to attend to another frozen moment, to leave its mark and to circle back or bolt forward

This is an ode, a celebration, an honor to the only thing that matters

To the only thing . . .

October 8, 2013

A feather wafted across my path

Golden lilting

It wistfully floated by catching the tip of my nose

It whirled and twirled and settled timidly

Lifting in the gentle breeze

Hail beat at my window, I feared the new nest would be lost

To the fierce beatdown of cables whipping against the

Drainpipe

The feather fell

Soggy at my feet

Dripping

It caught the light of the moon through the clouds

Shimmering delicate

Delicate unbent

Unbent

March27, 2014

A fern

I couldn't hold it

I lay a fern at its feet

I cried tears deep hollow from a place that old women cry

Who have seen things, known love, joy

Lost children

It felt like that

I tried to bury it

The fern may grow

Nourished by a past

I lay a fern green childish

I lay a fern in a daze

Hopeful that one day a tree will spring forth

Bearing sturdy oak and pink balloons

January 26, 2015

A great ship majestic of sail

Reached the shore glorious in bow and ornate in its aged wood beams

It glided smoothly over rock and coral

Of all colors waving tenderly as her belly slid by

The mist was golden soaking the masts with shimmering ore

Her bounty hidden beauteous and rare

She sailed in dark of blackest night. Her crew the ghosts of every voyage ever taken

Men and women who knew the way and never told their stories

They set sail by moonbeam and star and fine rudder

Silent only in silence did she sail to

Reach a shore of such rarity all trace of her gone now—a phantom of majesty and ore

No trace of her lies below the coral beds. No trace of her under the full moonlight

She told her story to the solitary foghorn that awaits her return at daybreak

She told her captain she would stand strong underneath him as the waves gouged beam and sail

Yet no one ever spoke of it or discovered her remains of

That voyage so rare underneath the moonbeams

October 22, 2013

If tenderness were a flower

What color would it be

Would it have a name beyond

Literal meaning

Can I carve it into my breath bleeding

Bleeding birth mandarin purple

Deep violet with golden tips

Could I return it then

From whence it came

I tried, I tried, I tried so hard

To express the colors that came from my shoulder

The tip of the ink ran down my notch

It called your name or three given

Three given

In light, in dark, in shadows, and sunrise

They were given because the colors were poignant, wistful

Shy perhaps, delayed perhaps

Or was it really perfect as it was

Spring came; the colors were fading against the harsh sunlight

Nest building not mine

Pine canyon hummers zoomed in to tell me not to give in, not to give up

They were listening. They always listened. We caught one for a milisecond

Hovering, warning, listening in dappling peridot

Dappling against the harsh sunlight reflected from waves of longing

Centuries of longing

Crashing into each other for respite, with joy, with lavender tips

More green than have ever seen in underwater expression

A sacred fire was lit and the flower on my shoulder had a name

She was named for tenderness

Given by the same

She bowed her head

Tears running down her jugular

Tears pouring across her shoulder

She would hold her head to the moon at dusk

She would ask the earth to hold her strong

She could smell the wind change

Tuck herself in

Watching for rain listening in the shadow

March 24, 2014

1001

It is a new year
On its way I prepare
I take out the sequined jacket gifted years ago
It fits now. My breasts grew into it like my heart filled
I imagine the softness of ivory silk against them
Caressing them as softly as the brilliance of the yellow and green paillettes on the shoulders
It is very grown up, very rock
It solidifies a truth in my past, witnessed, and honest
Like the photograph complete with signature that says I was really there
And so were you
I will twirl through the advent of the new year announcing 1001
I knew you then. Sunrise somewhere will also confirm it
As we walk barefoot in my cashmere robe dragging through the sand and salt
Before I return to where costumes serve the purpose I requested
I will have touched 1001 in my paillettes
Guided by the memory of where reality actually is

December 30, 2013

birth

High in the trees, mosquito nets surrounding

The mats where she slept

Her belly full

Lips swollen

Inside all was quiet

A poem turned

He held his ear against her navel and waited for the

Question mark to subside

She held him ripe oozing

A poem turned

It stretched wiping sleep from its eyes

Stumbling around for an opening it shoved

All the way into her heart

He held his ear against her navel

Waiting

November 8, 2013

Black smoke. Tossing

Tossing, tossing

Curled around a hot fire, I dream of longshoreman

Black smoke and molting shipwrecks

I want to document everything with the bus driver at

The end of the line and my camera

The news awaits my shots and I am unsure why this

Catastrophe or where

Tossing, tossing

Curled around molten steel, molten steel

Surges under a bridge to a town I do not know

The driver is game, just him and me and big glass windows

All the better to get the shot

A catastrophe I can't make out

But I want to document every moment no injuries just

Heat and smoke and raging fire

Raging against my lens and I miss nothing from every angle

My driver and I on this shiny new bus with gold fiberglass seats

He is up for my adventure thrilled to share this moment into the blackest hell

There are no people here but they talk to me by phone with the latest updates

Neither of us know why but we are running to it because I am there

Always there. It seems someone is confident of that

Blue train cars half-melted piled up against soggy roads unfinished or destroyed

We rush to this factory of black smoke confident for something important and needed there

No matter why, no matter why

Oct 31, 2013

The case of the missing spirit

Brring briiiiiiing

911

I wanna report a theft

Somebody stole my spirit

Excuse me?

I know she took it

Took what?

I know exactly when it was stolen

Laughter . . . Was it wrapped? Did it have a card? Laughter

Look, I did not even have a gift table

How do you know who sent it? Laughter

Because it is mine

What did it look like?

Look . . . I don't need a card . . . did not have a gift table . . . I just know that bitch took it

Look . . . sir . . . ok . . . describe it

Describe it? I know she stole it . . . cause it was a gift . . . Gimme a supervisor . . . cause I am not leaving

here until I get some answers . . . till I get some assistance

Supervisor: Can I help you?

A spirit was stolen from me . . . and I need some help

Have you tried the library? This is 91 . . . What is your emergency? A spirit was stolen from me—no card . . . no . . . I do not know who it was from, but I have some idea and I will

be taken seriously . . .

Hello . . . hello . . . are you listening to me? I demand a return of my spirit . . . and *she* has got it
Look . . . sir . . . not sure I can help but maybe the library can assist you. . . . Click

411

Hello . . . hello . . . this the library . . . i need some answers . . . because someone has stolen my spirit . . . 911 is not taking me seriously . . . I

What source can I help you with?

Well . . . I usually just pluck off info from the people around me. Easy peasy. No effort. They never notice I just took a little taste of their lives . . . I mean . . . after all, I can do what I like . . . If I want it, I just go get it. And no one. No one tells me no cause I always get what I want and that is just the fucking way it is

Listen . . . um . . . hello . . . sourcing . . . hmm . . . have you tried the second floor? Maybe they can give you some answers

Don't be a smartass . . . I tried 911. Not getting any results there. Now I have to listen to your crap . . . I need some answers and I am not leaving here until I get it . . . Period . . . And maybe I will just kill you . . . I do not like your attitude. How dare you not take me seriously? I always get what I want because I am someone who is somewhat important and you do not understand how it is to deal with me. You will see how I am a force to be reckoned with

Hello . . . have you tried the second floor? And anyway . . . what was the question?

I demand to know how come no one liked me. Why they refuse to answer my questions . . . and why is

everyone pretending they do not know how important I really am?

Look, sir . . . I can send you to the second floor . . . I can send you to someone who will help you

Screaming . . . sobbing . . . twisting of phone cords . . . twisting of phone cords and strange mental

telepathy . . . that further insists on being heard . . . You know I have the capability to kill you with my

mind . . . I will electrocute you throughout three existences and continents and I will make you tell me

what I want to know . . . Bla-bla-bla . . . beep beep beep beep

Cruising Facebook . . . face . . . how dare she . . . see . . . there it is . . . *my* spirit . . . .she stole it. I knew it . . . I knew it . . . I will keep looking because I *knew* she stole it . . . There it is . . .I can see it in her eyes. It belongs to me . . . and I will not stop until I get it. I will watch the posts and I will *know* she still has

it . . . What? There it is . . . that bitch . . . I will not leave here until she releases that spirit to me . . . It

belongs to me . . . I can see it in her face and I will take it back . . . It was given to me. It belongs to me. It is mine

It is mine . . . and always will be and I will not leave here until it is returned

2014

Cataclysms

Happen every day

Small things an electrical blowout of

Some kind

A tire, the wrong printer, the

Socks are separate colors

Shoes are off

Too much jewelry

Maybe

She has the same dress oh shit

Or wants what you want and cannot have it

Cataclysmic

Every day

But there is a seismic shift in the earth of my

Mind

A life plate that rolled over and shattered cracked the glass

Gave up, gave in, and screamed

Weeping with relief gratitude

A seismic shift of a larger kind

With soft colors pastel notions

And a dive at sea; oh land, you should be jealous

Youreallydon'tknowthemysteryofthegreensbluesturquoisegoldorange

Indelible ink

Staggering around without paper, paper, paper
Confused about the stroke of a fountain pen in the air
And when it met the cradle, again it laughed
For where the earth shifted was nowhere near
And the blossoms that wafted had just begun to open
The cataclysm moaned, turned
And called out the name it called out
And feet sank deeply more so and bells sounded no alarms
The silence confirmed it
With honor

March 15, 2014

Charcoal chartreuse

Radiant yellow

The palest of lavender with a touch of pink

These are my colors smoldering

Colors that you brought me

How is that this orb is so different

Each circle now filled in

Would it be awry to suggest

May I suggest

May I ask it

I decided against it

I swallowed it whole

Until it was whole

I marked it

I marked every corner with my personal label

I labeled it

I tied the box up tightly for safe delivery

The label said

Return to me

Special delivery

It arrived in silence on a sunny day or night I wasn't sure

Time stopped

The label was clear

March 15, 2014

Come here

I have stories to tell you

Stories of past and longing and mysteries

Come closer; I am speaking to you

Hidden here among the seaweed and the dampness

Tiptoe in, I must say this to you

Did you know, didn't you know

Why did you not know

Come closer

Ease in as gently as you can so I can whisper it

I must tell you this tiny story

It is so small it may elude you if you cannot listen carefully

It is red and orange and blue

Blue for most of the time

Bright chartreuse sometimes because I like it

Mauve hidden in mauve

It is angular and soft all at once; it has covered itself for lifetimes

Protective

It demands that you hear the story; now it is whispering, whispering

I came closer to hear a tiny story because it waved a tiny greeting

I was listening; I discovered I had always listened

So I sat down with the story while it sang and danced and wrote poetry

It described a journey of harrowing escapes and great failures and subterfuge

It told me of near complete defeat

I heard the story this time

Because I had one to tell

We told each other the stories in whispers

Of near failure and defeat and circles and subterfuge

We sang songs of victories and loss; we laughed great belly laughs

We honored the stories we each had to share

In a moment, in one eternal moment

We set each story aloft in whispers and the glistening damp

From lost to returned to blue sky to green wave to mysterious earthen clay

Red where my footsteps left notes and direction as to how the baskets must be woven

And how to catch a pomegranate seed for the best harvest

The stories took flight among the clouds and the cold and the dreariness of everyday

Set free on the wind and a wing too powerful, no hesitation

Set alight in flame to reach across oceans circling the moon and the sun

It whispered

January 6, 2014

Fall

Her costumes are particularly grand for November's ball
Matted, rusted iron groans heavily from the furthest branch
Burnished grape leaves twirl betraying the fanciful harvest they boast of beneath pungent earth
I am mad about the shocking red bleeding from the uppermost branch in a defiant last hurrah
The earth's last ball
Until everything is covered in white and silver blankets
Sleep, sleep deeply to thrill me with spring finery that inevitably comes
That inevitably reminds me of eternity
And for now, autumn's costumes are particularly grand

October 21, 2013

February Blues

It snows

And snows

Blowing against my staircase

The storm inside has quieted yet another day

I am certain

I know this for certain

The plows grind by in a dream

Squirrels forage intently under the snow

I am calmed by such gentility in the falling

Each one whispering its own vivid description

Asking me to choose my favorite

Reminding me of the difference

And it is identical

Still snow plush and damp

I dream of sunny climes and picture windows

My face pressed against the coolness searching for a footstep on cobblestone

Turquoise and black reveries and flowers for my hair

I will saddle up that pony out back my blankets sure

Into snow dreams

February 5, 2014

First snow

Insistent fragile

Each snowflake is named after you

Or I

Dependent upon whose eyes see them

The air betrayed me, no warning this time

They melt as they hit the earth rehearsing for the winter

As geese take flight rotating in pairs of ancient loves

Fragile hearty because they remind me that there is endless rotation in

The grand scheme of things and endless time

Even in suspension until next season

Peers across the horizon of rebirth anew

November 11, 2013

How do you put out a fire

Long burning high and bright
You light candles
Stoke the flames higher than ever before
Dig in deeper
Throw glitter in
Stack the logs side by side
Come rain or come shine
Thunder
I lit a candle
To an eternal flame
Just because
And that is all there is

May 6, 2014

I am not at home

I belong to no one and no place

I am possessed of things unimagined

I am alone

I live nowhere and everywhere; the world belongs to me

But not I to it

It loves me in tiny bits of spare time delayed, devotion to other concerns

So I belong to no one, no where

I am free . . . and yet what is the price for holding myself in

I adjust. I can shut down. I can knit my way furiously to a thousand scarves to give away to those who belong elsewhere and need more still to hold

I will stop giving. That is all. I belong to no one and I am free.

It is easier . . . as the world belongs to me and me alone . . . every corner is mine to explore

I can amuse myself as I watch and wonder whose spare time I am observing, and what little is left for me

I hate spare time. Where is that on the clock? Spareteen. Is that it? Let me check my watch again

I will not knit forever. I am easily amused by stories of others . . . while I create my own

I will dance my way to the next celebration . . . this time, I will entertain myself as I watch those
In their spare time . . .
Tick tick tock

January 2015

I grieve you

My bell a hollow place that held a burning so contemplative

So red and golden

I grieve you hot tears scorching my landscape that allows for no sound

It is navy blue and orange and sears me until I

I. I. I. Am lost in it

I almost enjoy that I have turned to stone

A slab of concrete

Step on it, smash it to bits with your well wishes

Take a hammer and carve up each last piece and pulverize it to ashes

Sprinkle it across the river that wanders between this life and the next one so I

I. May gather the shards of bone and recreate it

I cannot, cannot see, think, hear anything but the dust of a recollection

There are no more tears from this bone-dry carcass laid out to dry for vultures to pick at

Stolen from me by my own hand

Shelved. Colorless. Like the eyes I see through. Scorched barren from seeing too far for too long

Tethered to this lifetime in a promise that followed me from another life

I kept it all wrapped in a special color labeled with your name and mine

I broke the pieces one day to see if you could put them back together

I am scattered in the wind like the autumn leaves that circle the trees that lie in wait for spring

One tear more is too much to reawaken the granite that circles; two tears are not possible

From such a desert parched from frustration and ferocity

Forgive me do

I return to the cove where I sat in silence wrapped in this blackest mood near death

My shoulders shivering against the steel I self-created where once I turned inside and saw the sunrise

Stripped bare of pretense or shame, I now retreat behind this curtain a locked door of self-protection

In hopes a tiny butterfly will brave its way inside, tiptoeing gently in at my feet curious, daring ever so brave

To see what I am up to, whispering concern bravely before its life ends and it is reborn sending a message

Across the skies of hope and reconciliation from the butterfly tree that I have become

November 6, 2013

I Thought I Heard Your Voice in

The wind that raged outside my window

Rattling the shutters

Soothing at ease

Explaining why

Or how

I heard your voice against my cheek

As the howl and moan against the wooded window sill stood at attention

Listening carefully, I was disturbed

Gently disturbed as I heard the whisper again

Lower than the wind

A harmony in the cacophony

In the silence, another wind raged against me

I preferred it; tears streaming down my cheek, I could not speak

I responded with my entire being as I leaned against

Dripping tears against the wind and the silence that called my name

Closer, it pleaded, can you come here

Can you read the fine print underneath the window sill

I wrote my name with a flourish

I signed it with relish; I ringed it round and round again

I tried to absorb it and hold it closest of all for an eternity

Just three words is all

They were given against the tide of wind and salt and streaming tears

It was received and noted

mine

May 2014

I wanted it

More than chocolate

Silk stockings

A pair of new heels

Too high for my fractured

Ankle

Or pants too tight

That crush my belly

I wanted it

Most of all

For its ability

To elude me all

These years

It slid by

Taunted me

Left a familiar whiff

Somewhere I

Was supposed to recall

In my sleep

I wanted it

It showed up one day

Sat carefully nearby

Pondering my willingness

Cautious, hesitant
I eyed it through
Terrified lens
It crawled up on my lap
Peering suspiciously
We eyed each other
Sizing each other up
Feral ready to dash
Screaming
I offered it a tiny drink
A dew drop
It perked up
Listening to the air
And stayed

January 20, 2014

If I open like a flower

It is because you nurtured

Planted seeds of pure joy

A large dose of sun and laughter

A patient ear

A thoughtful eye that always praised

If I open like a flower

Each petal twirling into the sun by day

And the moon by night

It is because of you

It is because of you

June 24, 2014

If you lost yourself in me

I would drop breadcrumbs

For you to nibble on

Leave small trails of

Finite rays

Glimmering against my skin

To call you

I would return you to the hallowed place

You began

From the sacred journey you took

I would bring you home

June 2, 2014

In the spirit of decoration

He sat at some length outside my room

Or was it she that hopped and stood twitching on the step

In the first snow that seared my bones and my heart and reminded me that

Shoulders

Aren't just for port de bras

It was sleepless mostly the night on fire

Yes, fire scorched me, left me red burning; the leaves are covered now

And the first snow twirled in my heart and knocked on my door

While a bunny kept watch outside my window

I carved some initials on a tree whose roots had just been dropped

Anchor, anchor, where might you be

Maple or fir or the hearty pine that leave me breathless because it is decorated far more than just on

Holidays

November 26, 2013

It is bluer than I imagined

Tipped in icy green, the palest green at the tip of the ocean

It defies gravity or sunset

You can see through it to the bottom

Is it really the end or just the tip, the edge, the very edge

Of something even more lush, rich

Incoherent and light whispering of untold solace or danger

Does it flutter ever so pensive

Mounting an attack on the very solidity of blue and the

More well known

The palest of flutters not so wan as to be un-noticed

Insistent and birds flock to ascertain the secret in the deep

A pelican makes a mad dash hungry sure the treasure is captured

My footing slips on the very same mount

Climb I must to see beyond the shores beyond the sunset that ends the day but only the day

Nightfall, nightfall, night falls and divers succumb to the furthest edge in the sea of blues and greens

Against a hidden strip of protected landscape that breathes its own breath and tells its own stories that no one hears

The sea records them in silence spewing up small natives who rush into each other, blind and eager to find the source

Unimportant and substantial yet they feed each other until the next wave tumbles against their victories

Warning, warning of the precipice that lies at the edge where all take wing

October 21, 2013

Like a delicate brulee crust

I sliced through to the sumptuous

Flan underneath

I licked the spoon

Rolling burnt sugar on my tongue

It stung me

It melted

I was left with the taste of acid

Wine

Salivating, I pondered another bite

Questioned my reason for the spoon

Was the plate too small

I wanted to lick the plate

Repeatedly

Until it was gone

Drinking the caramel until it

Ran down my face like my tears

I slammed my spoon into the last bit of it

Wishing I had a fork for each sliver left behind

Wishing I had a fork

April 2, 2014

Listen to her spirit

Listen she learned

And a woman's spirit will tell you stories

It will tell you of the hurt and the exhaustion and the fight to survive

Without a word, it will tell you of victory

It says I struggle to go on another day

It will tell of love unfolding unfulfilled and sorrow

It asks for mercy or peace or

Whatever it needs to thrive on one more day

If you can reach into her heart

If you listen

You will find a universe filled with the jewel of comfort and warmth and ease

An ocean to envelop you in fine down wrapping you in unspeakable Tenderness

If you listen, you will hear her speak from the universe

She tells you her stories of loneliness and fear

Of resolution and joy, she will feed you from her table of riches

If you can listen, listen, listen to her spirit

It will whisper of halcyon days and nights where the land is plush and in full bloom

It will share treasures of gold and aquamarine and the finest you can behold

It will shed tears in joy and fear and absolute adoration

If you listen to her spirit and answer

Can you answer? What will you answer if she asks

She will ask

Lucky seven

What someone said when
You play craps blackjack
Or roll the di against the curb for street fun
One roll
You are broke washed up belly up on the sidewalk wondering what happened
I was inspired
Who knew what the last roll held
How uncommon were the stakes
I dug in my life
And lay one last dollar on the curb
I rolled lucky seven
This game had new rules, very old stakes, and a bottle of
Champagne; I could not drink oysters; I could no longer wash down
Salty brine hitting the back of my throat
Swallowing hard, I rolled perhaps one last time
Lucky seven
What was the victory to be exact
I asked myself repeatedly until I had no answers
Only the turn of the di made it clear
Face up on the sidewalk breathing deeply my victory
The one last roll was every bit worth the toss

November 11, 2013

Melancholy is a good word

To describe how the snow was flung up
Icy, gray, dingy, and balled
On my sidewalk
It was a delicate pallet this morning
I wanted to make snow angels in its purity
Something felt lost in this white blanket
Something that was good, real
The tow trucks lined the street
To carry off those who forgot
Lingering too long is problematic only for those
Who reside in lands where . . . air by nature is solid
And feet take root

January 3, 2014

It is Monday

An otherwise ordinary day

A day where sluggish bodies

And thoughts

Take their rest

And a fever settles into the

Pillows and car seats

The to-do list looms

The garbage awaits

It is Monday, an ordinary day

Where Proust and coffee raise their heads

December 16, 2013

A chill slid across my heart and this harbinger tore open a stream of assaults

I forbade it with a duel, a test

In my victory, my small pistol smoked quietly in the air

Still afire, who really lost today

A reclaim in a temporary coup de tat

Words are crisp, I limped across the battlefield

I rolled against the muddy carcasses of defeat and longing

I crawled across the molding hay and ash and pulled myself under the cover

Of dusk and dawn

Something changed. I am me. I. Am. Not we. Are them. Nous sommes

Nous sommes

And it is the only thing that matters

Ocean

It is Wednesday

I bring you into me by determination imagination

I am a plainsman

I do not forget the lessons you taught me that I bring here

The guidance you gave me with your song

You are the ease in my step, the ferocity of my temper

The depth of my being that no one sees because they only know the flatlands

Not the rolling crags covered with ice-plant and delicate flower

Or bulbous seaweed regurgitated from the moon at harvest time

Do you know the smell of garlic and artichoke and pear in black earth? So dark, so lush

You would eat it to take the smell inside you to be forever part of it

I am a plainsman now

I know the Indian trails; my moccasins uncovered the banks where orchards grew and I was warned to protect it

I heard the song and I remembered it; I remembered my promise to protect the land where my ancestors camped and wove baskets to carry fruit on journeys that left blood so deep it colored rivers

I will keep my promise to the plains with the lessons taught to me by oceans

I carry the salty dark earth of rolling farmland and dusky vineyards inside me

The kiss of an otter and the heritage of painters, jewelers, craftsman well up

You are in my footstep as I keep my promise to the plains you call me

You are wherever I am

You are the indigo blue in my brown eye and the fog that crosses me

I peer through familiar haze relieved by the damp and my hair stands on end electric

I step across the portal between sea and cornfield

Awash in brittle light and leafy welcome

Each feeds the other

And I take the lessons you have taught me here as I walk the plains where my ancestors wove their baskets

My step damp from seaweed and seagull droppings and rich damp earth

My basket full of the gourds left behind, I step forward with lessons from you

Your song guiding me across the plains

October 8, 2013

My table is filled

With Dates, figs
Pomegranates
I have dipped them
All
I have soaked them
In rose petals
Her juices cascade
Filling the bowls
As fruit swims
It is never enough
I split the fig
And roll each seed
On my tongue carefully
I am drowning in rose
It is the most delicate
Pink
Blushing near palest
Ivory
Pink nonetheless
Aghast shy
Softest red is tasted
In each small
Seed of date, fig, and

Pome apple

The palest rose

With the heart of lushes red

I circle my table

Gently testing

Its fruits

Outside the sun

Smiles wanly

Its fare not lost

Its fare a

Harvest a tribute

Mostly uneaten

Peaked in desire

Relished in

Solitude

An honorarium

To day

And night when

The palest pink

Fragrance

Lazily bleeds

Bleeds blackest red suet

And covers me

Under the still of

The moon . . .

October 11, 2013

offering

What would I bring you

Baskets of peonies and roses

All my stories unabridged

My honesty

The ship I sailed on which brought me back

My ancestors' footsteps that guided me through each forest

Showing me the poison from the riches under the moss

What could I bring you to lay at your feet

Peonies and roses and the smell of incense and galbanum from across the seas

Where I survived until this moment

Here I am with my little basket on my lap

In hopes that you recognize the treasure in my small offering

In hopes this is enough, enough

November 2, 2013

One, two, three

Kisses for thee

To myself I am true

Four, five, six

Loves me in excess

Tiptoeing across the road

A gentle plea

Spoke to me

And sent me a flower

A bouquet, a basket

Treasures unseen

I wanted them

I wanted them all

I shall tuck them deeply inside my inner pocket

Peeping in secret

One, two, three

Kisses for thee

My inner pocket

February 5, 2014

Poem one and two

It's raining

Each drop whispers as it winds

Its way through fallen leaves that mark my path

My path

Cushioned delicate, no longer cautious

It rains

The knocking at my windowpane is insistent

I hear, I hear everything

The answer was clear as a bell as the leaves swirled

Small tidepools welled up pushing against the grass

Demanding a reply, swelling, closing a circle in the damp yard

Long dormant

Green again for a day until the earth freezes her secret longings

Held in suspense another season

Held in suspense until a glimmer of light reopens a sleeping door

A sleeping door whose rusty hinges crept open for a tiny moment to capture the last raindrop

Before snow falls and writes another story of magic blankets

Blankets to seal the

tender seedlings awaiting the first kiss of spring

October 31, 2013

Today is a special day

Marred once by the pain of a highway robbery

Where I lost myself to an intruder who stole my memories of all I held dear

Left me beached for two weeks belly up in the darkness trying to find my way back

It changed today because I wanted it

Replaced in the rain and the sumptuousness of autumn air

It lifted a scar so deep I accepted it would never heal my badge of honor

I lit a candle to it and willed it away. I fought it bragging to others of its survival

From telling its story

It changed today; the landscape changed as did the air I breathe in

Something circled around my heart and played a gentle tune

That lulled me suggesting there was no longer a place for gashes in my mind

Or screaming stories of victory over the robbery

All that I lost returned to me and sat at my feet, weary of the journey too long gone

No words need be said to something that belongs and always did

How do I explain the relief for re-emerging intact

Did you have a nice trip—must I ask

I find there is no need; we both got lost and it was unnecessary

It slides back into place with ease twirling around like a comfortable shoe worn

Knowing it is still favored, it offers golden rewards for my stamina and fortitude

Sighing that it is welcome and I, I, I am truly victorious

I will remember the birthday I lost in the costume foray

The holiday that still mystifies me I got it wrong

The explanation faulty as to why the confusion is unimportant now

The puzzle fits tightly; the hem is stitched tight enough to hold it back in place

The thief that stole me that day is vanquished; no more stories to tell in my room as

The air rushed in the windows; blew open the curtains swinging gently against my teacup

Against my teacup

October 31, 2013

Prestige

Where is that
Your head filled with how that is supposed to look but
You can't take it with you
I care that you have it because confidence might be poking out from small shadows
It needs a spanking to remind it of its true less importance in the final scheme of things
Location
Who might that be and how does it look
Is it smaller than bigger than more closeted or free
It is only as important as the humanity at its center
Don't make me remind you that
Adornment
How much was it
Who does that matter to and who cares
Not as much as they do and who might they be
Are you naked enough and can you really impress me with that
Honesty
Taupe sand and sea glass, a dolphin welcome
A broken mug and dishwater coffee, a pinecone, a sand dollar
Rescued from the edge
I would wear it and listen to its song each night

October 31 2013

Red

I stood in front of it

Head on it, barreled for me hot

Catapulted from a heavenly crane it landed

Splattering across my chest and spread to the far corners of every part

Of the small universe I inhabited

It laid melting glass across a sea of regret and sorrow

It spilled over edges and took them along as it continued

To sear crevices left abandoned without rain or gold or even sandpaper

I staggered in my dreams calling for concern I could not breathe under

The weight of it I was blinded; I was left pressed against a wall

Where a door slammed and left me there

To hold this vermillion flame that I wrapped around myself in defeat

And was grateful for it

Grateful

November 8, 2013

Curled across a chest

From memory

Blind touch

An open box that held

A tray

Musty old relic

Such that it was

Those boots still danced

January 21, 2014

She was a treasure

For a moment

A brief moment she was captured

Honored

She wore a wreath of laurel, an olive branch extended

She feared it was a temporary tribute to love gone by

Never realized, never spoken

Her yearning laid page after page

At the foot of this mountain

It snowed, it rained

In some parts of the world, the tides rose higher than normal

Birds flew and spoke, sang songs for the first time

Songs that did not call to their mates, songs of longing

Something new

An aberration from the call because no mate responded; the nest remained empty

She adjusted her crown that allowed her to write sonnets no one would hear

They eased her pain for a tiny time; she set fire to each page and sent ashes to the sky

For one tiny moment in time, she saw herself trying to breathe in the essence of something

That forever eluded her

She tried to inhale it, capture, close the lid on the bottle she put in her pocket

Her breast told her the truth

You are alone it said and no one can hear you anymore invisible

Choices were made; choices are made every day

The tears came hot dry, squeaking down her cheek

Her chest aching cold again where for one tiny moment, she was a treasure

Her name was new like her skin; her toes curled, each one reflecting how it felt

To touch cashmere and silk across her arch

She had raced forward to capture the illusion

Every hair that twirled around a beloved sphere alive with honor and joy

Frozen in some kind of pathway to the past, the future not sure

But she was in it wondering when someone would smash the glass and claim the prize

It did not appear she was the winner

She piled up her tributes in the little bonfire

She knelt at its feet to ask why

And how this managed to happen

She lit her torch and remembered

And she would burn the name into her arm

When she set her flame alight

March 10, 2014

Sorcerer

A wand was waved and I obeyed

Driven by the magic in its tip

Commanded woven against a sky of stars

So brilliant they shamed the sun

Embellished the moon

And took them both on a journey that set the

Earth against its own rotation

I peeked out daring to challenge the spell

That lay heavy across my shoulders

A stellar bit of most tender thorns

Joined against the rose that bent her head ever so

She wept

She wept tears of dew and honey and arched against the steel

That melted against the strap that constrained her

A wand waved and driven in its tip

Was a magic never heard of from a far-off land

With a common name that no one ever whispered

No one

January 18, 2014

Special delivery

A flower was delivered by express

No card no vase was needed

A wispy leaf hung from the stem

A facsimile I am told

My heart hurt sometimes but I had this wilting flower

I kept pressed in my memory

Reminding me, reminding me

Of a time when invisible things were made tangible one afternoon

Perfectly clear for someone who was so blind for such a long time you see

Every nuance can be clearly read, every tear a silent joke

Am I holding my own hand or is it a dream

I want to say I thought the curtain's edge pressed against my cheek

I want to say I caught a whiff of orange blossom and tangerine wafting by

It was no longer summer's edge

Fruits and resins and the heady scent of crisp leaves replaced it

The outline of a curve against my pillow

I close my eyes and send letters long unwritten

I send letters in invisible ink and I close my eye and I thought there were three

December 3, 2013

Spring and the feathers floated across the yard

The headless bird separated from its body
Where it lost the fight to survive against an assault
That beckoned in the vicious circle of life and death
I swept the remaining pieces of it
I said a prayer and imagined the wings took flight
Across my back yard once again
The flight of the free and pure
The flight of a life re-imagined
The baby sparrows sang heralding
New life, new joy, a song
A song to the dawn of peace

April 25, 2014

Stop here, she said

I want to show you the town I love

That talks to me adorned in feathers and boots

That holds me tightly so I cannot breathe sometimes

That pulverizes me into rubies and diamonds

It is not a birthday

It could be

Let me show you the town I love

A whale spoke to me there to assure me

She was not lost after all

The driftwood haunts me with grey twists and turns that match unpainted fences

Salt pure salty fog takes care of that

The hamlet I love has secret coves covered in Indian blankets and saris

Arms of bangles and kurta of turquoise

No one goes there unless you have the key

I will show you the hamlet I love

Cobblestones in hidden corridors and buried treasures unearthed at sunrise

A cypress pretends to sleep at the precipice

And the moss opens her arms and speaks your name because

She remembers your junior high path cut through the sands

That never open to the public; no fences, no gates

Wildflowers planted for your hair of rarest breed and where iceplant

Celebrate autumn

November 4, 2013

The call

I heard the call

From deep in the apple orchard this morning as birds flew

The call of the young coyote who has lost his first mate

A poignant song of reverie loss and celebration

A song of celebration

He thanks her

A small drum beats magnolia flowers through her heart

As she moves away

Across the sky over the apple orchards where they discovered each other

She will rise to greet him in the dawn and watch from the moon

He will call her for a lifetime in memory and she will answer

I do . . .

November 3, 2013

The end of an era

Of dreams a fantasy

A mirage that took me to a brief oasis

In a desert

A desert I passed through only once before

You were at the edge

Still running as fast as you could

Running to where is uncertain

We found our way to a small watering hole

Discovering that shared nourishment can be important and brief

We made our way through the caravan

Of lovers and more conquests

Lost hopes recovered dashed again

The sun shone hot overhead

I emerged

June 16, 2014

The photos have no meaning

They no longer speak to me

Tell me the truth

Of loss, hurt, pain

It is in the eyes they say

Regret for the future

For a past

For this realization that it was

Just a passing fancy

Never set free

Set free today by one's choice

I shall write tributes to this thing that never

To a thing that never

To a thing that never

Seemed if only in a dream

I cannot put my finger on why

Do you deserve sonnets, reams of sonnets

Mystified completely mysterious

Not really because you knew, refused once again

Tired, frustrated, I give up, I give in

I concede to my loss, oh yes

I am supposed to find peace

But I shall wander and hold a candle to every
Every being that passes my way and I shall ask
If it is you I shall ask, is it you

March 17, 2014

I can turn three minutes into

Three thousand years in a life second

Freeze it into crystal

And hang it in the light to spin

Colors bouncing through the air

My eyes exploding from the fusion of mystery

Hope and memory

I can turn three minutes into three thousand years

Simmering in a pot of bouillabaisse

Each morsel a fragrant tip on my tongue

Exquisitely designed to burst from each corner on the inside of a cheek

Leaving its mark in flavor and hue

I can swallow its song as it crescendos to a crest on the wave

Of the thousand years where cranes fly together

Celebrating the arc of the next thousand

Each minute a tribute to the other

Covered in feathers, covered in the kimono that journals my voyage

I can recall each second that leads to the second thousand

Pulling from me floating frozen in my hand

The tiniest infinite pads against which I hold a moment, each moment

Reeling against resistance with slightest effort and fondest

Fondest, fondest, most sacred most holy
Open, open again to feel the stars flash across a palm
Catching my breath as it curls around fading into a ball in front of a flame
Imperceptible, barely imperceptible, so tender it is imagination
I can wrap three thousand years in three minutes
Of longing and curiosity
I heard the exclamation beyond the question
I heard the end of the sentence and the declaration
I heard beyond the cool and the chill and some finality that made me want to stomp out the last
Fire
I wept for each second
Crashing into a wall of denial
I re-emerged for another thousand years
This is for every artisan relishing love
And for all who follow here . . .

March 5, 2014

Under the deep

We swam into crystal clear coves and bulbous kelp

I ran my hand against barnacles

Gasping at the sheer realization of small things in the universe

I could breathe the air without a mask

I swam where I could not

Hearts pounding in the quiet, I smelled salty air

A school rode by and danced for only me

Was it stingray that slid by uncertain if I belonged there

I heard only the gentle rocking, gentle rocking, yes I heard it

I heard only the sound of my heartbeat in the crystal deep pale green

Against a mask that breathed for me

A fin, a flipper, I could not swim but I dove beyond a place of memory under a deep green crystal

Soothed in quiet, in a place I forever call my home

December 10, 2013

Under the magnolia tree

It was buried deep

The mask familiar

Yet stripped away

Under the magnolia tree

Strength glided down the concrete

At ease on land as in

Sea

Mercurial languid

Reluctant

The mask was transparent

It hid the longing

It hid fear

The petals dropped from

A solitary magnolia

Fragrant pure

Delicate

The mask slid away

A sigh of relief

Roared across

The sand dunes

January 20, 2014

Under the boxwood

She ran dashing around in circles

The boxwood part of the fortress she built in her castle grounds to protect herself

From fire ants and dragonflies and the hunting dogs lounging around the corner

They watched over her, actually, reserving ferocity for the small rabbit or bird that flew by

She knew them well . . . on this day, they watched over her as she circled the yard

Looking for clues . . . searching for fairies, they came for tea and orange soda; she drank on the sly

Arches too high . . . she ran barefoot as fast as she could in her silk dress so no one could see

She was really the queen of all; she surveyed under the redwood ledge of her nana's house

She sat under the window, contemplating the smell of Chanel from her grandmother's room

Her auntie came to the door with Chanel and Pierre . . . a poodle who would never fit in with the guards of the back yard

He was banished for being too fine, but the bottle of number five stayed

She rummaged around dressing up in it, decorating herself in finery that seemed appropriate on days

When fairies came to visit

And when she grew . . . she always understood that

Pixies were everywhere

And magic was still possible

If she only believed and never forgot the days of boxwood and ants and dragonflies

Under the redwood ledge

December 12, 2013

The unmade bed

Rumpled from yesterday's love

The beams watched tenderly from above

Pensive

The unmade bed

Her scarf lay at the end

Gazing at the lonely fireplace

She would go home

She would go home to solitude and reverie

Taking the beams and the window view with her in her heart

It was Christmas time and handmade ornaments warned of exhausted hands

The departure loomed

Three . . . two years in the making or more

She stayed behind hopefully

A journey of her own to take that brought her back to a room with a fire

The view spanned decades and ten thousand years behind

She would tuck the corners in, carefully taking up time to prolong a moment

She would curl each pillow case thoughtfully smoothing the corners

Wrapping the frail blanket tenderly alongside the rug where her shoes sat

Cautious ever prepared to run

Run anywhere, anywhere, but found herself by the fire that raged

from the log that burned too fast

Unlike that evening, that solitary evening, where the bed

Lay unmade . . .

November 8, 2013

Volcanic ash spewed

From black sand beaches hot
Oily hidden among frangipani and oranges
The sunrise inflamed by the tender shoots left
In the wake of lava long stored underground
I dove, I dove, where I could not swim
Breathless, disarmed by the beauty of a long-forgotten age
It was crystal clear peridot with turquoise glimmers
I remembered how to swim and my shoulders pushed against a soft wave
Tapping, tapping against the coral bed, I was welcomed into a sea of unknown depth
No undertow to diminish a life rediscovered, no beach to fall back into for safety
A waft of frangipani told me the name of the cove I discovered
It left on the breeze as it arrived
A pearl fell from the shell that presented itself
I rolled it gently in my hand, admiring the glimmers of it in the sunlight
A story never told whispered in the peacock and olive hues a touch of indigo

The sun set, the sun set, one last time and I clutching my tiny pearl strode
Across black sand in the moonlight

January 6, 2014

You digest

Think long and hard

Really very easy

I am not so cool

Too much energy to tamp down the heat

I do declare

Casually

Causally

Mull it over like a warm blanket

It is alright I live

No regrets . . . I am free

Butterfly flitting

Only a few hours to soar

I run into the flame risking all

I am not so cool

You digest or ignore

Mull it over or block it out

I thank you.

May 6, 2014

www.ingramcontent.com/pod-product-compliance
Lightning Source LLC
Chambersburg PA
CBHW021450070526
44577CB00002B/339